HAYES PRESS

Spiritual Warfare: Satan and His Kingdom

This book was professionally typeset on Reedsy.
Find out more at reedsy.com

Contents

1

SATAN'S GREATNESS AND FALL
(KEITH DORRICOTT)

Every disciple of the Lord Jesus is affected by the person of Satan, who although a spiritual being and invisible to us, is nevertheless a very real adversary. The Bible refers to him and his actions repeatedly, yet we will search in vain for a complete explanation of his beginning.

Satan, in the form of a serpent, first comes to our attention in Genesis chapter 3, where we read of the fall of man. He tempted the new creature to sin in the same way as he himself had done, and so cause the sin which was in him to enter the human creation. It seems clear therefore that a great deal had happened in Satan's history before the events in Eden, but we are told very little of this, - obviously for our own good. "The secret things belong unto the LORD our God: but the things that are revealed belong unto us" (Deuteronomy 29:29). What has been revealed is that:

1. Satan was created in the original creation of the angels,

   which preceded the creation of man;
2. his was the first evil aspiration; and
3. this had enormous consequences for the entire creation.

Let us look at what Scripture reveals about each of these.

Satan's Origin

Satan is not a divine being. He is an angel - a spirit being created by God. The creation of angels preceded the work of creation that is described in detail in Genesis chapters 1 and 2; by how long, we do not know. But Job 38:6,7 tells us that the angels (who are described as sons of God) witnessed the laying of the foundations of the earth. And yet they too were created because all things in the heavens and upon the earth, visible and invisible, were created by God (Colossians 1:16).

The angelic creation is vast It consists of innumerable hosts. Angels are not a multitude without distinction or order, Scripture tells us that there are angelic principalities and powers (Ephesians 6:12). They are organized into legions, as human armies are (Matthew 26:53). Some have particular responsibilities on this earth - for example: for children (Matthew 18:10) and for the nation of Israel (Daniel 12:1). At the head of this great hierarchy are those angels who have the rank of archangel (Jude 9). And the greatest of all at the beginning, it seems, was one called Lucifer.

Almost all of what we know specifically about Satan's origin has to be inferred from two passages of Scripture. The first is in

Ezekiel 28:12-19 and speaks allegorically about the king of Tyre. The second is in Isaiah 14:12-17. The name Lucifer means "son of the morning". He was the model of created perfection. He is described in the Ezekiel scripture as:

1. being "full of wisdom";
2. being "perfect in beauty"; and
3. having the highest responsibility as "the anointed cherub."

Satan's Fall

How long this state of sinlessness lasted we do not know. But then came sin. And it began, not with the least of the creation of God, but with Lucifer, for Ezekiel 28 tells us that:

1. his wisdom was corrupted;
2. his beauty gave rise to pride in his heart; and
3. he became no longer satisfied with his mighty position under God.

It is extremely significant that the root cause of this first sin was pride. What initiated it, or why God allowed it, we do not fully know. Lucifer had been blameless, but now wickedness was found in him. It was the wickedness of pride - of self-centredness. He said "I will ascend into heaven, I will exalt my throne above the stars of God; I will sit ... I will ascend above the heights ... I will be like the Most High" (Isaiah 14:13,14).

Perhaps we can get an insight into this momentous event by contrasting Satan with God the Son. The Lord Jesus Christ, as God the Son, was and is superior to all angels (Hebrews 1:4,6).

God the Father, according to His eternal purpose, has appointed Christ to become heir of all things (Hebrews 1:2).How much of this eternal purpose Lucifer knew because of his privileged position we do not know. But Lucifer certainly coveted the position and authority of Deity, and so, being a created angel, he intended to exalt himself to become as God. He was therefore cast down (Luke 10:18) under the judgement of God - the inevitable result of pride (1 Timothy 3:6). What a contrast to the Lord Jesus who, being God, humbled Himself to become lower than the angels (Heb. 2:9) and so was exalted by God (Phil. 2:9)! "Every one that exalteth himself shall be humbled; but he that humbleth himself shall be exalted" (Luke 18:14).

The Result of Satan's Fall

Often, in the ways of God, there is both an immediate and a future result. For example, in the case of our salvation, we are born again now but are not freed from sin until we leave this body. So with Lucifer's sin. Pride and self-centredness cannot exist for a moment in the presence of God. For Lucifer, judgement ensued (Ezekiel 28:16) which Christ Himself witnessed (Luke 10:18). He was no longer Lucifer but "Satan" (i.e. the adversary) and "the devil" (i.e. the deceiver). And so the age-long conflict between the Creator and the greatest of His created beings, now sadly corrupted, had begun. It was to involve many hosts of the angels, it was to involve the entire human race, and it was to involve the very Son of God.

It seems that Satan was not alone in his revolt but was in fact the leader of a great multitude of the spirit beings. Ephesians 6:12 speaks of "the spiritual hosts of wickedness in the heavenly places" and Jude 6 refers to "angels which kept not their own principality" and are kept for future judgement. Thus Satan has his own angels - those demons who were so active during Christ's lifetime on this earth (Matthew 12:26).

During his temptation of Jesus in the wilderness, Satan claimed that all the authority and glory of the kingdoms of the world had been delivered to him (Luke 4:6). He has enormous power, for even the archangel Michael would not rebuke him (Jude 9). And so Satan's domain is no longer the presence of God but the earth (Revelation 2:13) and the air (Ephesians 2:2). Until the time of his future judgement, God allows him to exercise power, so that God's purposes may be completed. And so Satan still has access to God (e.g. Job 1; Zechariah 3:1). "The whole world lieth in the evil one" (1 John 5:19).

For Satan and his angels there is no repentance. Christ did not come to save angels but mankind (Hebrews 2:14-18). And so Satan is relentless in his opposition to God and to His purposes for mankind. Satan is still determined to be "as the Most High", to "ascend into heaven", and "to exalt his throne above the stars of God". But God has prepared for him and for his angels a lake of fire which burns for ever and ever (Matthew 25:41). This is our adversary: not flesh and blood, but intensely real.

2

SATAN AND THE FALL OF MAN (GEOFF HYDON)

In considering this fundamental part of divine revelation we can usefully examine the issues involved under four main headings; dealing with the character of the Deceiver, the initial environment of man, the circumstances of the Fall, and its consequences (the latter being divided into negative and positive aspects).

The Serpent

The principal characteristic of Satan is found in his name, which originally meant adversary. In his opposition to God and man we first find him in Bible revelation described as the Serpent. This title is confined mainly to the books of Genesis and Revelation and is usually linked to his work as the arch-deceiver (Genesis 3; Revelation 12:9; 20:10). In this his character contrasts diametrically with that of God who cannot lie (Hebrews 6:18).

In this series of studies we have already seen how evil was first manifested in pride in the heart of Lucifer. For the present purpose we may simply state that a wholly righteous God was clearly not responsible for the evil attributes of the creature in the Garden of Eden, the serpent. Moreover it would seem correct to assume that the deadly venom of the serpent now present in its nature is a development of Satanic involvement (Luke 10:18, 19), not a faculty that was present in its original constitution, seeing that death was experientially unknown until the Fall. We may conjecture that the subtle character of the serpent led Satan to choose that creature for his physical embodiment in Eden, but Scripture does not record whether that choice was made solely by the Evil one or with the acquiescence of God (compare Matthew 8:32). Nor does it explain the ability of the serpent to communicate effectively with the woman.

As a general scriptural principle we are expected simply to exercise faith in what God has seen fit to record of the matter. One thing is clear from that record, the fall of man was conceived and precipitated by the wily intervention of the Deceiver in God's perfect creation. Thus the Serpent was allowed to bring the spiritual powerplay of evil against good into the realm of mankind.

The Scene

The effects of the Serpent's work in the Garden of Eden can only be judged properly when account is taken of the original creation, which bore the seal of God's approval (Genesis 1:31). Everything was good, in terms both of man's environment and, more importantly, of his relationship with God his Maker. All that man required to satisfy him: sustenance, authority and companionship, were provided (Genesis 1:28,29; 2:24). Moreover, communion with God was a privilege enjoyed by Adam and Eve, as indicated in Genesis 3:8-9. What a wonderful revelation of God's will and work must have been theirs! They viewed with sinless eyes the wonders of a perfect creation. The holy, omnipotent, and loving character of God must have been clearly visible to them (Romans 1:20) in a way that transcended even the experience of the psalmist, who, despite the taint of sin could yet witness to the magnificence of God's creation (Psalm 19:1-6).

The Fall

Into this glorious scene comes the arch-deceiver, the Serpent, with a triple temptation to thoroughly beguile Eve (2 Corinthians 11:3). There is a subtle difference of degree between doubt and disbelief which is starkly brought before us in the account of the Fall in the contrast between the Serpent's words to Eve, "hath God said?", and his further statement "ye shall not surely die", the latter containing the prompting simply to disbelieve. He first planted the doubt, then suggested advantages if only Eve would disbelieve. In the same way we often are guided by his wiles to "just try", on the basis of doubts as to whether a course of action is really wrong. Which of us can point an accusing finger at Eve? In her case the Serpent's three-pronged attack was quickly completed when he prompted her, in view of the apparent benefits, to take the fruit (Genesis 3:5).

In this connection the statements of 1 John 2:16 have often been compared to Eve's response to the tempter; the lusts of the flesh and the eyes and the vainglory of life being linked to her view of the fruit as (i) food; (ii) a delight to look upon, and (iii) being desired to make wise. How the course of our history would have been changed if she had fed on the food of God's ordinance, looked away to view God's handiwork, and satisfied herself with the wisdom of doing His will! But her initial resistance to the Tempter (Genesis 3:3) soon melted away. Maybe it was Adam who had told Eve not so much as to touch the fruit; he after all was the one to receive the command-even before Eve's creation (Genesis 2:17).

Perhaps the instruction was repeated directly by God to Eve. By whatever means she received the proscribing words they were disastrously unheeded. Adam was not likewise beguiled (1 Timothy 2:14). As a consequence of the events that had taken place he had simply to decide, of his God-given freewill, his course of action. His sin was outright disobedience of the holy command - the result of his deliberate judgement

The Negative Consequences

At that point the Serpent had apparently accomplished his objective. He had successfully struck at the whole of God's earthly creation by striking at its head - Adam. The venom of his deadly bite would now pass to all earth's inhabitants causing death (Romans 5:12), which in man's case had a twofold aspect: a primary break in his relationship with God and a secondary spoiling of the physical harmony of man and his environment.

While rampant sin would soon have its disastrous effects, the initial changes resulted from the righteous judgements of God. The ideal surroundings of the Garden were put out of bounds.

The ground was cursed, changing man's enjoyable labour to arduous toil. Mental and physical anguish began, as evidenced by Adam's and Eve's hiding from God (Genesis 3:10), and God's statement to Eve concerning childbirth (Genesis 3:16). Subsequently, man's dominion over the animal kingdom was disturbed; killing and being killed came to be parts of a new natural law of survival, and animals had to be put to death to meet the physical and spiritual needs of man (Genesis 3:21; 4:4). Death had entered the world, and in its primary form it cut the links between man and God (as evidenced by the ejection from the Garden and the need for sacrifices in order to approach God thenceforward).

Clearly, God's pronouncement as to the punishment of death in Genesis 2:17 had wider significance than the cessation of Adam's heartbeat and respiration. Death in that physical sense was to occur much later (Genesis 5:5), although the biological process of ageing immediately began. Physical obstacles to communion as a result of expulsion from the Garden were subsequent to a spiritual break in the relationship between Adam and God, which caused the man to hide from his Maker as a result of his sin. It is this spiritual 'death' to which God was principally referring when giving Adam the command concerning the Tree of Knowledge. We may describe such a severe break in communion as death. Consider for a moment what it is that first suggests to us the death of almost any living thing. It is the lack of response. We sense that something has occurred which has cut off all lines of communication and we describe that circumstance as death. So God said that Adam would die, in the sense of being separated spiritually from God and lacking in response to Him, even whilst his blood was still coursing through his veins. The root of the problem lay not in his heartbeat but in his heart condition, in the change of his very nature which governed his attitude towards God.

Resulting from that change is the propensity to sin which we see in ourselves today. Man had a God-given ability to decide either to obey or disobey the command of God and that ability has progressively been exercised in disobedience since the Fall. Vigorous attempts by individuals and groups throughout history to prove that man can cleanse his character if his surroundings are improved have been doomed to failure because of the continuing work of the Deceiver, who caused the basic change in man's nature to occur. When Satan struck at Adam he had in view not only changing Adam's nature and staining his character, but the marring of God's creation for all time.

How close he came to success because of the inexorable transmission of sin by Adam to all his race! For surely we now take our characteristics from the fallen nature of Adam (Romans 5:19; 1 Corinthians 15:22,48). We now sin because we are born sinners (Psalm 51:5; Romans 3:10; Ephesians 2:1). Death in Eden was so far-reaching. The effects on us of the Serpent's attack are awfully reflected in Galatians 5:19-21 where the term "the flesh" describes the disposition of the fallen nature. As we may envisage how a child's hands once disobediently plunged into the paint pot will lead to marks of that paint in every quarter of the child's activity, so we conclude that a fallen nature will result, in varying degrees, in works of the flesh.

The Positive Consequences

The Fall was a seeming victory for the Serpent, but what of the positive consequences? The reference to the "Lamb … slain from the foundation of the world" in Revelation 13:8 indicates that God in His foreknowledge had planned to circumvent the Serpent's activity in the Garden. Hence the triumphant statements in Genesis 2:24 and 3:15. The first of these verses could not fully apply to motherless Adam himself, but was directed to his race. It foreshadowed, moreover, the relationship of Christ and his Church (Ephesians 5:31-32) which would surpass even the initial bliss of Adam and Eve in their sinless state. The Second Man exercised His freewill in perfect submission to His God and Father. That unique obedience accomplished a perfect salvation, and also provides for a perfect unity between Christ and His Church. Man had a testing point for his obedience - the tree of knowledge - and he failed, but in doing so proved that he possessed true freewill, a freewill that could have been exercised in obedience to God (as was demonstrated by the Son of Man).

The final testing point for the Lord Jesus came at Calvary, where Satan attacked the Head of all Creation. But the Serpent's head was bruised and Christ, as progenitor of a new race, gives new life and a new nature to those who become His seed. This triumph brings, and will bring, glory to God in Christ - the eternal purpose of creation (Colossians 1:16-18). Those who believe in the Lord Jesus Christ today can glorify God by surrendering their will, the right to do as they please, to His will. This logically makes them prime targets for attack by the subtle Serpent who despises the victories of the garden of Gethsemane and the Cross. We rejoice, however, that in subjection to God we can resist the Deceiver and he will now flee from us (James 4:7-8).

3

SATAN'S MOTIVES AND METHODS (KEITH DORRICOTT)

Motives

Satan's name itself gives us the key to his motives. Satan means "the adversary". John the apostle said (in 1 John 3:8) "the devil sinneth from the beginning". From the beginning when he was cast out of heaven, Satan set himself up in opposition to God and to God's purposes. Satan is the archenemy of God. And so the primary object of Satan's enmity is not Christians, or even unbelievers, but rather God Himself. He has not repented of his aspirations to God's throne and he is relentless in his pursuit of them. Expressions throughout Scripture such as, "as a roaring lion, walketh about" (1 Peter 5:8) and "straightway cometh Satan" (Mark 4:15) give us some idea of the never-ending activity of Satan in opposition to God. Why does God allow it? Surely it is within God's power right now to banish Satan to the lake of fire, which has specifically been prepared for him (Matthew 25:41). So why is it that Satan is allowed the power that he has?

In the answer to this question we are given a glimpse of the marvellous sovereign works of God. Psalm 76:10 tells us that God makes even the wrath of men to praise Him as He did in the case of Pharaoh (Exodus 9:16). And similarly God permits Satan a degree of power over the human creation for His own divine purpose. We see it in the experiences of Job, of Peter and of the Lord Jesus Himself. The words of Joseph, you "meant evil against me; but God meant it for good" (Genesis 50:20) illustrate this principle. And so Satan's objective is to destroy (1 Peter 5:8) – to destroy anything for God – which is why he is so active in the spiritual affairs of people on this earth; for God's eternal purpose revolves around people. Christ did not "take hold" of the seed of angels but of the seed of Abraham (Hebrews 2:16). God chose us (not angels) in Christ before the foundation of the world (Ephesians 1:4).

Thus, because we are so central to the purpose and pleasure of God, Satan focuses his attacks on us. In the case of unbelievers who hear the gospel, Satan's purpose is clear. He who works in the children of disobedience (Ephesians 2:2) blinds "the minds of the unbelieving, that the light of the gospel... should not dawn upon them" (2 Corinthians 4:4). And so the gospel preacher may present Christ in a very clear way, but the sinner cannot see it. He is being hindered by the adversary. As the word of God is sown, the devil, like the birds of the air with seed, takes it away so that there might not be any life as a result (Mark 4:15). In the Gospels we see also Satan's influence over men – to the extent of demon possession. For example, the poor man who was called "Legion" in Luke 8:30 was possessed of many demons - presumably those angels who were associated with Satan in his great fall from heaven - and it took the authority of Christ to release him. Then again, the lady with the blood disease for twelve years is referred to as having been bound by Satan (Luke 13:16). And Satan's greatest power is the power of death, for Hebrews 2:14 describes him as "him that had the power of death".

With the believer - whether the Old Testament man or woman of faith or a Christian today - Satan's objectives are the same - to destroy anything of value for God. In the case of Job in the Old Testament, we are allowed to witness a scene in heaven - God holding forth Job as a shining example of faith and Satan on the other hand seeking to destroy that faith by doing everything within the powers granted to him by God on that occasion (Job 1,2). Satan's purpose? To destroy Job; God's purpose? To prove (and improve) him. This opposition takes place in the very presence of God.

In the case of the Lord's disciples in the New Testament, Jesus said to them (Luke 22:31) "Satan asked to have you, that he might sift you as wheat". And then He said to Peter in particular, "but I have prayed for thee, that thy faith fail not: and do thou, when once thou hast turned again, stablish thy brethren". Satan's desire was to destroy; the Lord's desire was to preserve and to enable Peter, by this experience, to be strengthened for his future work. Satan meant it for evil; God meant it for good. And so God uses even the evil motives and enmity of Satan to His own divine ends. He is indeed the Almighty.

Methods

Satan's other name is the Devil, meaning "the deceiver". This gives us the key to his methods. Satan rarely attacks overtly or obviously - because this stiffens resistance. But he appears as an "angel of light" (2 Corinthians 11:14). What a contrast between his real activity (as a roaring lion) and his appearance (as an angel of light)! During the life of Christ we have only one instance recorded of direct Satanic attack - in the confrontation in the wilderness after the Lord's baptism (Luke 4). But several times and in various indirect ways, Satan used other people in his opposition - such as, king Herod in the murder of the infants at the Lord's birth (Matthew 2:16), the Pharisees (John 8:44), Peter (Mark 8:33) and Judas Iscariot (John 13:2).

Ephesians 6:11 warns us against the wiles of the devil. 2 Corinthians 2:11 tells us "we are not ignorant of his devices" What then are his methods? One of Satan's primary powers is his ability to tempt us. Take the case of Judas in John 13. Verse 2 says "the devil having already put into the heart of Judas. . . to betray Him". Then verse 27 says "then entered Satan into him". A great deal happened between these two verses. First, Judas was tempted by Satan. But temptation is not sin; Satan can provoke us to sin yet cannot make us sin. But temptation leads to sin if we harbour it and foster it (James 1:14,15) - and this is what Judas did, with the result that his greed for money caused him to betray the Son of God. But James says in his epistle (4:7) "resist the devil, and he will flee from you". How is it possible that Satan will flee from us? Only because of Christ's victory over him at Calvary. Christ "brought to nought him that had the power of death, that is the devil" (Hebrews 2:14). In Christ's name, we are to resist Satan's advances.

One of Satan's primary weapons is his relentlessness. When resisted by Christ in the wilderness, he departed from Him - "for a season". Satan may be resisted but he will return - using all the attractions of the world (the occult, entertainment, sexual perversion, materialism, peer pressure, etc.) to appeal through our senses visually and aurally to our natural lusts of pride, greed, ambition, curiosity, self-gratification, etc. He is the father of lies (John 8:44) - making things seem to be what they are not, making what is wrong appear right. As Peter said to Ananias in Acts 5:3, "why hath Satan filled thy heart to lie to the Holy Spirit?" We are never exempt from his attacks and never finished with them. In the New Testament epistles specific instances are given as to how Satan tempts various classes of believers:

1. he tempts husbands and wives to become selfish in their relationship with each other (1 Corinthians 7:5);
2. he entices overseers to be impressed with their own importance (1 Timothy 3:6);
3. and saints to hold a grudge (2 Corinthians 2:10,11).

In such cases Satan's stock in trade is deception. We are frequently not conscious that he is behind the temptation. Realizing this is vital. How often have we all felt hindrances to our spending time in scriptural reading and prayer? Defeating the enemy of God can only occur through the divine power available to us (Ephesians 6:10-18).

"Faint not, Christian, though the road

Leading to thy blest abode
Darksome be and dangerous too;
Christ, thy Guide, will bring thee through.
Faint not, Christian, though in rage
Satan doth thy soul engage;
Take thee faith's anointed shield,
Bear it to the battlefield."

4

SATAN: THE PRINCE OF THE POWER OF THE AIR (DON McCUBBIN)

Satan is described on several occasions as a prince (John 12:31,14:30; Ephesians 2:2), and he is called Beelzebub, a name of doubtful origin, but which means the prince of demons (Matthew 12:24); in addition he is the god of this age (2 Corinthians 4:4). Thus he is in a position of considerable power and authority with a kingdom that was attested by the Lord Jesus, who said "if Satan... is divided against himself, how shall his kingdom stand" (Luke 11:18). However Satan is never called a king, because nowhere is his authority absolute. His kingdom is not hell, as many have popularly supposed (Dante, Milton), but it is the kingdom of darkness (Colossians 1:13), which is in opposition to the kingdom of God. Satan thus rules over both unregenerate mankind and the multitude of demons.

When certain angels revolted against God they were cast down to hell, that is Tartarus, and they remain there in bonds until the day of judgement (2 Peter 2:4; Jude 6), so they are restrained from further evil activity. Many other spirits have rebelled, but

God in His wisdom has allowed them to retain their freedom, and to act as minions of Satan and assist in his nefarious activities.

"The prince of the power of the air" is a unique expression (Ephesians 2:2), and the form of the language in the original Greek is unusual. The phrase is therefore rather difficult to interpret, and various explanations have been given by commentators from the early Church fathers onwards. It would not be profitable to reiterate all these opinions, as many can only be described as ingenious and fanciful. One common interpretation is based on the word used here for air (Greek: aer), which means the lower air or mist, as opposed to the upper clear air (Greek: aither); thus the lower air has been equated with the darkness, but the usage seems more specific. The air does not here mean the ordinary physical atmosphere, nor does it imply that the earth is literally surrounded by the hosts of Satan.

"The power" (Greek: exousia) it should be noted means a delegated authority; Satan is not omnipotent. The preferred meaning of the expression 'the power of the air' would be the authority over the sphere of activity where the hosts of wickedness operate. This corresponds to the spiritual hosts of wickedness in the heavenly places (Ephesians 6:12). Thus the air is parallel in thought to the world (Greek: kosmos), with air representing the spirits, as the world represents unregenerate mankind, both of whom are under the power and influence of the evil one. The prince and all his demons are totally united in opposing the purposes of God, and directing against Him the affairs of the sons of disobedience.

The tragedy is that mankind is naturally blind not only to the light of the gospel, but also to the existence of demons and their evil influence. Demons are also called evil, unclean or familiar spirits, and sometimes incorrectly called devils. Since there is no reproduction among spirits it would seem that each one had individually rebelled against God and given his allegiance to Satan; or, it has been suggested, they may have originally been subject to Satan and then defected together at his fall.

The kingdom of Satan seeks to copy the universal kingdom of God. For as the latter has a hierarchy of thrones, dominions, principalities and powers (Colossians 1:16), the former seeks to imitate with a rival organization of principalities, powers, world rulers and spiritual hosts of wickedness (Ephesians 6:12). It would be difficult and highly speculative to define each of the above terms separately, or even to differentiate precisely their functions, but it is evident that there are two great forces working in opposition, one for good and one for evil. While God has provided the highest good for mankind, Satan is deploying his forces to hold down fallen mankind and encourage men in selfish greed, ambition and the other works of the flesh, and indeed all that is hostile to the will of God.

Nature of Demons

- they are spirits, having no material form, but they seem to desire physical contact, perhaps to give them greater means of expressing themselves (Matthew 1:43; 8:31).
- they are personal and have names (Mark 5:9).
- they are intelligent and possess powers of thought, speech and action, and they can distinguish between true and false

(Acts 19:15).

- they believe in God, but show no repentance, and they also recognize the deity of Christ (James 2:19; Luke 4:34).
- they have some knowledge of the future as they are aware of their destiny (Matthew 8:29).
- they exhibit degrees of wickedness, since some are described as more wicked than others (Matthew 12:45).
- they are able to enter human beings and animals, but the mode of access is unknown.
- they can voluntarily leave a possessed person and later return (Luke 11:24).
- they can afflict both physical and mental disabilities on their victims (Matthew 12:22; Acts 16:16 ff).
- they are powerful and can exert supernatural strength in their victims (Matthew 8:28)
- they can display emotions, such as fear and rage (Luke 8:31).
- they can be exorcised by the power of God, however some are more difficult to expel than others (Mark 9:28ff), but in any case only a minute fraction of His power is needed, as is expressed by the finger of God (Luke 11:20).
- they can influence people without possessing them (1 John 4:1).

Activities of Demons

These activities consist of both opposing the purposes of God and extending the authority of Satan. The scope of their work has varied from time to time depending on the strategy of Satan, who can assume many guises from that of a roaring lion to an angel of light. Perhaps deceit is the most common characteristic. While these activities reached unprecedented levels in New

Testament times, as Satan mustered all his forces to oppose Christ, there is ample evidence of the work of evil powers in the Old Testament.

The evil practices of the Canaanites were fostered by the powers, and no doubt Satan specially directed his forces to corrupt the Israelites as they came to possess their promised land. There were severe warnings in the Mosaic Law against evil practices and also making sacrifices to idols, which were effectively offered to demons (Deuteronomy 32:17; Psalm 106:36ff). For though the idols were nothing in themselves and completely powerless, they became potent through the demons. Later Paul confirms that offerings to idols are sacrifices to demons (1 Corinthians 10:20). The corruption was very extensive involving human sacrifices, soothsaying, sorcery, spiritism, divination and necromancy; those who practised these things were to be cut off from the people, and sometimes condemned to death (Leviticus 19 and 20).

King Saul, who had previously removed those with familiar spirits and wizards from the land, turned in desperation to the witch of Endor when pressed by the army of the Philistines, after Samuel was dead and Saul had lost contact with God. The woman, under pressure from Saul, sought her familiar spirit, but she was terrified when instead the spirit of Samuel appeared. This clearly shows that the spirit of a deceased person does not normally appear at a seance even though this may be claimed to take place. The sentence on Saul is a solemn warning to those who would indulge in the occult. (1 Chronicles 10:13). Evil spirits were sometimes used by God for His own purposes, which demonstrates His overall power; for instance God sent an evil spirit between Abimelech and the men of Shechem (Judges 9:23), and a lying spirit was used to punish king Ahab (1 Kings 22:23).

All departure from God led inevitably to idolatry, as shown by Jeroboam, who ordained priests for high places and for demons (2 Chronicles 11:15). Evil spirits were much in evidence in the occult practices of the wicked king Manasseh (2 Kings 21:6ff). The continuation of these practices led some of the prophets to give specific warnings against spiritism, as they looked forward to the future cleansing of the people and the day when all evil would be banished from the land (Isaiah 8:19; Jeremiah 27:9ff).

The Gospel records present a very clear exposure of the activity of demons, with many references to the healing of those possessed by demons. The effect of demon possession is manifested in different ways as the victims variously exhibit insanity and mental disorders (Matthew 8:28), or blindness, dumbness, epilepsy and other physical afflictions (Matthew 17:15). Some victims appeared to recognize that they were possessed, but they were in fact only acting as instruments of the spirit. Sometimes the evil spirits overruled the whole personality to produce complete mental confusion, as in the case of the Gadarene, who said "my name is legion; for we are many". The legion represented a considerable number of spirits, who changed the man into a maniac, but when they were expelled by Christ the man became completely normal; while the spirits in requesting entry to the swine seem to have vainly hoped to escape their coming judgement (Mark 5:1-20). It is most important to realize that not all sufferings were due to demons, for we are told that the Lord cast out demons and performed cures (Luke 13:32).

Demon possession was very wrongfully attributed by the Jews to John the Baptist because of his ascetic habits (Matthew 11:18), and to Jesus also when He said "If a man keep My word he shall never see death" (John 8:51ff), which they considered to be absurd. Some expositors have maintained that demon possession required at least the initial consent of the person involved, (e.g. A. H. Strong); but while this may sometimes be true it will not always be the case, since young children have been affected (Mark 7:24ff). While the death of Christ on the cross marked the sentence on the powers of evil (Colossians 2:15), God has still permitted them to operate until the future day of judgement. The practice of the occult was shown to be a lucrative occupation by three cases in the Acts - (a) Simon the sorcerer, who offered money to the apostles for the gift of laying on hands to receive the Holy Spirit (Acts 8:9-24), (b) the girl of Philippi, who brought much gain to her masters by soothsaying (Acts 16:16ff), and (c) those who practised magic arts at Ephesus, and whose books were valued at fifty thousand pieces of silver (Acts 19:19).

Since New Testament times there have been many references to the activities of demons by early Church teachers, such as Justin Martyr, Tertullian and Augustine, but some of the cases seem to be exaggerated. At the time of the Reformation there was a surge of demonic activity, which both Luther and Calvin recorded, and Calvin's treatment of the subject is particularly instructive. The current increasing fascination with spiritism and witchcraft is very disturbing.

We are told that "in later times some shall fall away from the faith, giving heed to seducing spirits and doctrines of demons"

(1 Timothy 4:1). There can be no doubt that seducing spirits are behind many modern cults, as they were behind the idols of old, so that these cults not only deny the existence of evil spirits, but they also attempt to refute many fundamental Christian doctrines. As Satan can disguise himself as an angel of light, so his minions can appear as servants of righteousness (2 Corinthians 11:14ff), to corrupt the truth and produce most palatable teachings, which are in reality doctrines of demons. The deceit knows no limits for even the fellowship of the Lord's table is counterfeited by the fellowship of the table of demons (1 Corinthians 10:21). For believers possession by demons is impossible, as regenerated persons are sealed with the Holy Spirit (Ephesians 1:13).

Though we are not immune from the attacks of the evil one, who is ever seeking to bring discredit on the work of God. God has provided us with a defence, and this is the subject of a later article in this series. Paul could write "we are not ignorant of his devices" (2 Corinthians 2:11), and we would pray that we all might be the same.

5

THE COURSE OF THIS WORLD (JIM RODGERS)

The word translated "world" (Greek: kosmos) in our English versions of Scripture means, literally, order (arrangement), or adornment, but it has a wider usage, as denoted in the following examples. It applies to the earth in its material structure as is evident from such passages as Matthew 25:34; "... the kingdom prepared for you from the foundation of the world"; John 1:10, "the world was made by Him" and Romans 1:20, "the creation of the world."

It is also used of the inhabitants of this earthly sphere in such scriptures as "For God so loved the world" (John 3:16); "Behold the Lamb of God, which taketh away the sin of the world" (John 1:29) and "He (the Holy Spirit)... will convict the world in respect of sin..." (John 1.6:8). These three passages portray the triune God in action in respect to the world - the earth's inhabitants. A specific segment of the world's inhabitants is referred to in 2 Peter 2:5 as "the world of the ungodly", and John 15:18,19, "... the world hateth you... ye are not of the world..." These passages indicate two types of people as being in the world. One class is termed "the world" who in turn hates the others who are "not of the world". The latter are looked upon as being in the world but not of it.

Finally, so far as our present study is concerned, there is a sense in which "the world" is used to denote that worldly system which affects mankind through the "... lust of the flesh, and the lust of the eyes, and the vainglory of life,..." "World" in the title of this chapter's subject has this last meaning and is found in Ephesians 2:2. With such a variety of meanings, the word "world" can be confusing as to the particular sense in which it is used in any given passage. It is necessary to apply one of the basic guidelines in scripture interpretation - the examination of the word in conjunction with its verse or passage context. Following this principle the word in Ephesians 2:2 is linked with Satan as "the prince of the power of the air". As such he is the instigator and controller of the course of this world. It has as its central objective opposition and disobedience to the will of God, and has a ready response in those who are termed "the sons of disobedience". "The course of this world" is clearly associated with what has previously been referred to as the "worldly system."

Previous chapters in this book have touched on Satan's aspiring to set his throne above the stars of God (see Isaiah 14:12–15). Pride was the root cause of his ambition (see Ezekiel 28:17), and characterized his subsequent actions and influences. Throughout the ages the methods employed, the pressures exerted, and the enticements offered by him have had the sole purpose of establishing things which would run contrary to the mind and will of God. An example of this is seen when he influenced men to "build us a city, and a tower, whose top may reach unto heaven", as recorded in Genesis 11. The resultant confusion, together with Satan's continuous change of methods and repetitive failure of plans, suggests that he has forethought but only limited foreknowledge.

The welding of the human race into a unified world system originated in the city men built in the land of Shinar (Genesis 11). Throughout the history of mankind Satan has used every conceivable device to advance that system of unity. Despite the variation of tactics the means employed can be summarized in the terms previously referred to in 1 John 2:16, "the lust of the flesh, and the lust of the eyes, and the vainglory of life."

It is impressive to note that Satan seems to have come full cycle from the land of Shinar (Genesis 11) and back again in the end times as described in Zechariah 5:5-11. This seems to indicate the limitation of his resources. He is back to the place where he commenced but is unwilling to admit defeat without one final supreme effort to unify the nations under his authority. This conglomerate, this world system, is represented in the woman named "Wickedness". It combines men worldwide in one secular and religious order for the purpose of world domination. This development is confirmed and amplified in other portions of Scripture (e.g. Revelation 18).

Of particular interest is the reference to the ephah in Zechariah 5. In some passages of Scripture the ephah refers to a divinely or-dered portion regulating measures for honest dealings amongst the Lord's people (see e.g. Leviticus 19:36). During a period of national declension in Israel, it is linked with the shekel, elsewhere named "the shekel of the sanctuary" (Amos 8:5). The people were far removed from the Lord and His ways. They impatiently longed for the time when they could ignore God-given guidance and engage in profitable commerce through dishonest dealings. This purpose is clear in their wanting to make "the ephah small, and the shekel great" - selling a lesser quantity for a higher and unjust price.

The Lord so abhors this flagrant disregarding of His laws governing the ephah and the shekel, that He summarizes the prevailing conditions as "dealing falsely with the balance of deceit". Whatever else is intended in the mention of the ephah in Zechariah 5:5-11, we judge it to be symbolic of Satan's usual counterfeit procedures. In Genesis 11 they had "brick for stone, and slime had they for mortar...", in Zechariah 5, he copies divine standards of righteousness. So effective are his methods that in these last days they will "lead astray, if possible, even the elect" (Matthew 24:24). The passages cited in Genesis 11 and Zechariah 5 touch on at least one aspect of Satan's designing and directing of the "course of this world", at early and end times.

The period between the two incidents referred to is over 4,000 years. A more detailed study would reveal repeated instances of Satan's tireless energies and efforts, throughout each dispensation, to overthrow the purposes of God. Embodied in these satanic activities down the centuries is what we have previously referred to in the New Testament term, "the course of this world". The study of the recorded effect of this upon individuals and communities during the 4,000-year period we necessarily leave with the reader.

Subtlety was ever Satan's hallmark (see Genesis 3). His approach is the lust of the flesh and the lust of the eyes, and the vainglory of life. Throughout the continuous changes affecting the dispensations he has accommodated his ways to suit the circumstances of that particular day. The course of this world specifically applies to the unregenerate, as indicated in Ephesians 2, by its link with the sons of disobedience. Repeated warnings against becoming involved in worldly things, together with warnings of Satan's activities against the believer (e.g. Ephesians 6:11), show that the attraction of the world is not confined to those who are blinded by the god of this age. The course of this world, in the present age, is overlaid with seemingly harmless things, hence the difficulties at times in discerning right from wrong.

It is mentioned in the passage in Ephesians 2 that believers have been made alive, they who had aforetime walked according to the course of this world. Why should they return to that from which they have been liberated? Peter graphically describes such a backward step as, "The dog turning to his own vomit again, and the sow that had washed to wallowing in the mire" (2 Peter 2:22). If, as so often seems to happen when faced with a choice of enjoying the world's offered attractions or otherwise, we have to ask what is wrong with them, it may be concluded that such are at least suspect and our participating in them open to question. It is not always possible to obtain a "thus saith the Lord" to all of our queries but, for balance to the previous question, would it not be advisable mentally to ask, "what is right with them"? The offered allurements, which cater for the flesh, are soul-withering and gradually rob the individual of his or her spiritual appetite.

The appeal of the world to each individual may be likened to the course of a river which at its source offers a refreshing change to the weary traveller. Its cooling waters for the moment quench the thirst, soothe the burning feet and are an aid in forgetting some of the trials of the journey. Following the stream, it gradually broadens and deepens until one can bathe in contentment, hardly conscious of the gentle motion which, with the river, carries all within it ever onward and downward. The thunder of the mighty cataract can be faintly heard in the distance but it creates no fear in the heart of the relaxed figure enjoying to the full what the waters have to offer. In less time than can be imagined the scene has changed.

The individual is suddenly aware of a stronger current and is alerted to the fact of the river banks being now so far away. The roar of the waterfall is no longer faint, or at a distance; it is time to make for safety. Too late! The current is far stronger than human energies, and the frail form, despite superhuman efforts, is caught up in the mighty hand of the swirling rushing waters and finally, in the uncontrollable power of that mighty cascade, carried over the brink to perish on the rocks beneath - another life lost. This is a simple analogy of a very important aspect of the course of this world. To tamper with worldly things is dangerous. At their source they seem so harmless and are easily controlled; but beware of what the future holds! The total of what the world offers is exceedingly underweight when placed in the balance against a spiritual life. We are reminded of this in the Lord's words, "what shall a man be profited, if he shall gain the whole world, and forfeit his life" (Matthew 16:26)?

It is appropriate to close this chapter with emphasis on the words recorded in 1 John 2:15, "Love not the world, neither the things that are in the world."

6

THE ACCUSER OF THE BRETHREN (LINDSAY PRASHER)

How often have we heard from gospel preachers that heaven is where no sin can enter? While this is true of the eternal state (Revelation 22:3, 15), Ephesians 6:12 speaks of "spiritual hosts of wickedness in heavenly places", or as the NIV has it, "spiritual forces of evil in the heavenly realms." One cannot escape the conclusion that in God's infinite wisdom, He allows access by forces of evil into the heavenlies. And there are examples of Satan approaching right into God's presence.

One example occurs in Zechariah chapter 3, where the prophet's fourth vision is recounted. He sees Joshua the High Priest of Israel standing in filthy clothes before an angel of God. The angel is told to replace the dirty garments with clean ones. The reason is not hard to find. The visions followed the end of the seventy years of captivity in Babylon and the return to worship in God's re-built temple in Jerusalem. In this vision the prophet was being prepared for the re-establishment of divine worship after the long lapse. It is against this backcloth that Satan is seen standing as an opponent right beside the angel and, as the voice of God was heard by the prophet directly addressing the Adversary, it would appear that the scene is set in heaven. Satan was out to stop the return to the true worship if he could.

However, God stepped in and in effect told Satan that he had fuelled the fire of departure of God's people long enough, but He had pulled out of the fire this burning stick and quenched it. God said that, though Joshua's clothes were dirty, they had now been made clean to serve Him in His new house in Jerusalem and nothing Satan could do would reverse it. Just as Satan did his best to prevent the return to collective worship according to the Law of Moses, which applied in Old Testament times, so today in New Testament times he endeavours to thwart collective worship in the house of God.

Another example of Satan's activity before God affects Christians as individuals, as distinct from their collective life, for in Revelation 12:10 our adversary is devastatingly described as the accuser of the brothers. This implies that when you or I do wrong things, Satan goes to God and draws attention to what we have done, asking whether God will own us when we do such things. So we must all be careful not to give our enemy the chance to run to God and point the accusing finger at us. The amazing feature of this situation is that, despite such accusation, if we are really sorry for our sin and tell God so, God will forgive us in His wonderful mercy. But how much better not to fall into wrong-doing in the first place, then we don't give our ruthless foe the opportunity which he relishes.

A third and outstanding example of Satan's action in God's

presence is found in the story of Job. It might be thought that, because Job was so upright and blameless and because he shunned evil, the adversary would have nothing to point the finger at. Yet such is the subtlety of Satan, his attack took the following line. He told God that it was easy for Job to be faithful because he had been given so many comforts and blessings. If these were removed, he would curse God to His face. Fully knowing what He was doing, God gave Satan permission to take away all Job's possessions, but not to touch the man himself. The story is well known, how his cattle and their herdsmen, his sheep and their shepherds, his camels and their attendants and even his sons and daughters were all killed in turn In all this Job sinned not nor charged God with foolishness.

The relentless foe did not stop at this. He appeared before God a second time and said, "Skin for skin, yea, all that a man hath will he give for his life. But put forth Thine hand now, and touch his bone and his flesh, and he will renounce Thee to Thy face". So God again allowed Satan to do what he wished except that Job's life must be spared. At this Satan caused boils to erupt all over Job's body. However, even when his wife said, "Renounce God, and die", Job's reply was, "Shall we receive good at the hand of God, and shall we not receive evil?" So the real trust that Job had in God shone out more strongly because of his terrible misfortunes and Satan's ploys proved quite ineffectual.

Instinctively we turn the spotlight from Job to ourselves and have to recognize that God allows Satan to afflict Christians at some time to some degree. The degree may vary from person to person, but what a comfort it is to know that God will not let you be tempted beyond what you can bear and will always provide a way out so that you can endure it (1 Corinthians 10:13). The inference is that Job must have been outstandingly strong spiritually or else God would not have allowed Satan to tempt him so sorely.

There was only one really perfect Man who lived totally to God's pleasing, and, while there is no record of Satan appearing before God in relation to the Lord Jesus, we do know he tempted Him at every turn, directly as during the forty days in the wilderness and indirectly through the action of men under the Devil's sway, culminating in the crucifixion at Calvary. Yet Calvary was the scene of Christ's triumph through suffering infinitely greater than Job's. Jesus gave up the spirit with the resounding cry, "It is finished". The adversary had certainly bruised the heel of the Seed of the woman, as God forecast to Adam and Eve, but himself received a head blow (Genesis 3.15). The truth of this was seen on the resurrection morning, when the Scripture reveals that, not only was His body raised from the tomb, but His soul left Sheol, taking captivity captive, having the keys of death and Hades formerly held by the adversary.

This is a fitting point at which to complete the Job story, for God recompensed the man who suffered so much under the hand of Satan, by giving him twice as much as he had formerly owned and prospered him with seven more sons and three more daughters, the fairest in all the land. So Christ, by His victory over Satan, at whose hand He suffered so much more, will be more than satisfied to see around His throne thousands who will be beautiful in His glory, and you and I can look forward to being among them, Praise His Name!

7

LIMITS OF SATANIC POWER (JOHN TERRELL)

"This is your hour, and the power of darkness" (Luke 22:53).

Circumstances most solemn surrounded those words of Christ. The conflict of the ages, with all the forces of hell in battle order, was about to reach its climax at Calvary. Anticipating His approaching decease the Lord declared, "Now is the judgement of this world: now shall the prince of this world be cast out" (John 12:31). Yet in a terrible sense it was "your hour, and the power of darkness"; an hour allowed, indeed ordained, by the sovereign God of salvation for the full deployment of every Satanic force against His holy Son.

We shall see that it was also at the cross that the ultimate, eternal limitation of Satan's power was effected; the final curb which enabled the apostle Paul to ring out the triumphant challenge, "O grave where is thy victory?"; and the redeemed of the Lord, with quiet confidence, to declare themselves "more than conquerors through Him that loved us" (Romans 8:37).

All down the ages of divine dealings with men and angels, however, there have been limits imposed by God upon the authority and powers of the devil. We may ponder the unrelenting judgement on certain disobedient celestial beings (Jude v.6); while at the same time observing the high standing and freedom of activity which divine omnipotence permitted to the adversary himself (Jude v.9). True, in God's perfect wisdom and judgement, the "covering cherub", having rebelled, was dispatched in summary fashion from his place of heavenly greatness. The Lord declared to His disciples, "I beheld Satan fallen as lightning from heaven" (Luke 10:18). Though the base of his evil operations could not be heaven itself, yet God allowed to him wide spheres of activity and influence as suggested by such terms as "prince of this world" and "prince of the power of the air"; while Satan's evil associates are designated in such sinister terms as "the world rulers of this darkness." And in a sense not elaborated in Scripture, the enemy had access to heaven as depicted in the book of Job.

Now it is, of course, the experience of this exemplary man of God which offers us one of the clearest and most penetrating insights into the matter of God limiting Satanic power. Without this exposure of God dealing on behalf of His own, many a faithful soul would have been crushed beyond endurance by overwhelming afflictions. What amazing confidence and trust God placed in His devout servant! And what a position of trust we occupy from day to day as those whom our Lord relies upon as His witnesses in the world, as "ambassadors on behalf of Christ". We must often confess that the "accuser of our brethren" is afforded more than ample material for his malignant purposes (Revelation 12:10); and our diligent Advocate is occasioned frequent exercise of His gracious intercessory service (1 John 2:1). In all of this the believer takes unfailing comfort from the knowledge of a sovereign hand upon the tempter and destroyer. The words of Job 2:6, "Behold, he is in thine hand" might well strike terror, until we reflect upon the Speaker who can add with unassailable authority, "only spare his life".

This glimpse behind the scenes of the dramatic suffering and testing of Job only exposes the more painfully how superficial and hollow were the subsequent words of Job's friends. So much so that, ultimately God intervened with, "Who is this that darkeneth counsel by words without knowledge?" (Job 38:2); and proceeded to declare in majestic poetry His everlasting creative power and glory. We see no more the dead hand of Satan, but the splendour of divine omnipotence. "Then Job answered the LORD, and said, I know that Thou canst do all things, and that no purpose of Thine can be restrained... I had heard of Thee by the hearing of the ear; but now mine eye seeth Thee" (Job 42:1,2,5). May suffering saints' eyes be opened like Job's, and those of the prophet Elisha's young man (2 Kings 6:17) to appreciate by faith the over-ruling hand of divine bye, power and wisdom.

To the Corinthians Paul offered the priceless assurance, "There hath no temptation taken you but such as man can bear: but God is faithful, who will not suffer you to be tempted above that ye are able; but will with the temptation make also the way of escape, that ye may be able to endure if' (1 Corinthians 10:13). At the same time it is well to note that in this passage the apostle is warning against yielding to temptations, although God has permitted them, so that there is both comfort and caution in the words.

We have briefly considered above the reality of direct divine intervention in the limitation of the devil's power. There is also another important sense in which God exercises control of Satan and his evil servants. We might reverently call this a purposeful manipulation of certain of the adversary's activities. In 1 Samuel 18:10 we read that, "an evil spirit from God came mightily upon Saul", and in 2 Corinthians 12:7 about Paul we read, "there was given me a thorn in the flesh, a messenger of Satan to buffet me". So in His dealings with these men, spiritually reprobate on the one hand and devoutly pious on the other, God had a positive hand in the deployment of essentially evil agencies. In the one case the rebellion of the heart was amply confirmed; in the other the triumph of grace was beautifully displayed. Thus yet another aspect of the over-ruling of a providential purpose is demonstrated in Satanic activity.

In all the annals of revelation, however, it is supremely in the Lord's earthly ministry that the limitation of Satan's authority is seen. Beginning with the wilderness temptations recounted in Luke 4, we witness the unfolding of spiritual resources for victorious living, to the glory of God. Here the Master points out the high way of spiritual conquest through the power of the Spirit and the living word of God: These represent the believer's principal armoury in conflict, and the only means of curbing the adversary's onslaughts. And how many hours of intensive supplication and prayer must have filled these long days of temptation for the Lord! His response to this, and to many subsequent episodes of severe temptation, provide us today with the finest example. Yet the Lord in His ministry also directly intervened in Satanic activity for its severe restraint. Most notably, of course, was the casting out of demons. "If I by the Spirit of God cast out demons, then is the kingdom of God come upon you" (Matthew 12:28). Indeed the Holy Spirit declares unmistakably in 1 John 3:8 that "to this end was the Son of God manifested, that He might destroy the works of the devil".

Now this appropriately returns us to the crowning limitation imposed by God upon the power of the enemy - the triumph of the Crucified. The casting out of the prince of this world (John 12:31) at the cross marked the beginning of the long, slow but relentless decline of Satan's powers towards the fearful climax of the lake of fire (Revelation 20:10). It was at the cross that, "having put off from Himself the principalities and the powers, He made a show of them openly, triumphing over them in it" (Colossians 2:15); and it is at the all-authoritative behest of the One who is "arrayed in a garment sprinkled with blood" and who "hath on His garment and on His thigh a name written, King of kings and Lord of lords" that the powerful angel lays hold on the dragon, the old serpent which is the devil and Satan and binds him in the abyss for a thousand years (Revelation 19:13, 16; 20:1-3). We glory in the incarnate Son who partook of flesh and blood "that through death He might bring to naught him that had the power of death, that is, the devil" (Hebrews 2:14). "O death, where is thy sting?"

Flowing gloriously from the victory of Calvary are all the eternal blessings of salvation for the believer. But the experience of conversion, of birth from above, itself entails an entirely new relationship to the adversary. Wittingly or unwittingly - or perhaps a bit of each – the unbeliever "walked according to the course of this world, according to the prince of the power of the air, of the spirit that now worketh in the sons of disobedience" (Ephesians 2:2). Now he is "quickened". Once he was the captive of the "power of darkness". Now he is "translated into the kingdom of the Son of His love" (Colossians 1:13). He is turned "from darkness to light, and from the power of Satan unto God" (Acts 26:18). Before he was a sinner bound for eternal judgement; now he is a member of "My church" against which "the gates of Hades shall not prevail" (Matthew 16:18). He is sealed with the Holy Spirit of promise unto the redemption of God's own possession (Ephesians 1:13,14). Never will he, or can he, be sealed, as will some, to eternal destruction (Revelation 14:9,10).

Throughout the Christian life there is a solemn responsibility upon the believer to be acutely aware of the devices of the adversary (2 Corinthians 2:11); to be alert and watchful against the "roaring lion" who "walketh about, seeking whom he may devour" (1 Peter 5:8); to resolutely deploy "the whole armour of God" in the unending struggle against the "spiritual hosts of wickedness in the heavenly places" (Ephesians 6:10–17); to resist the devil and see him flee from us (James 4:7). In such ways we can, by God's help, vastly restrict and limit the power of the adversary for evil in our lives. In Romans 7 we see something of the struggle Paul knew and in Romans 8 the overcoming power of the indwelling Spirit is expounded.

Brief reference has already been made to the end-time activities of the enemy and to the limitations put upon them. This repeatedly features in the Revelation narrative. For example, in the matter of the seals, the trumpets and the bowls, we see at certain points how the Almighty, through His strong angels, unleashes some of the forces of Satanic horror (e.g. Revelation 9:111) as judgement upon a rebellious earth - all under strict heavenly control. Again, in Revelation 12:7-17 we see the deceiver of the whole world granted certain powers in a well-defined location as precisely decreed by a sovereign God, and similarly restricted as to time - "knowing that he hath but a short time" (Revelation 12:12). And so to the awful final judgement leading up to the new heaven and the new earth.

In Revelation 20 is recorded the final outcome of the death-stroke inflicted at Calvary, when the old serpent is bound, then loosed again and finally cast into the lake of fire. With such certainty before and such examples as Job behind, the child of God can rest in the confident assurance of divine supremacy and sovereignty. He can reflect in holy fear that, in the midst of his temptations and afflictions, perhaps a voice full of understanding and of trust is challenging the enemy, "Hast thou considered my servant...?" Every lift of the evil one's finger is under God's unerring control; and the captivity of His own is ready to be turned, as was Job's, just at the moment decreed by divine wisdom and love (Job 42:10).

8

SATANISM TODAY (PETER HICKLING)

A fair title? The use of the word 'Satanism' might be thought deprecatory from the beginning, and rather like using the word 'Papist' in an article about Roman Catholics. Many of those who practise the things discussed in this article would deny that there is any connection between them and the worship of Satan. Nevertheless, it is contended that all practices of witchcraft, spiritism and magic (except, of course, the entertainers' tricks called 'magic') involve intercourse with spirits who owe allegiance to Satan, and thus are forms of Satanism, even though their practitioners may not recognize the fact. For the purpose of discussion, however, it is useful to differentiate between those who consider that their practices are good, or at least morally neutral, like scientific research, and those who deliberately cultivate evil.

Magical practices

A practitioner of magic has given the primary meaning of the term as "the art and science of using little known natural forces in order to achieve changes in consciousness and the physical environment". It involves such things as the invocation of gods, the evocation of spirits and ritual divination. Its devotees dedicate themselves to magical studies with an oath which promises "not to debase my knowledge of practical magic to purposes of evil", but one formula of evocation recognizes that the spirits addressed are 'infernal', and some writers almost dismiss the existence of evil.

There is considerable difference between writers on these matters in the ways in which they regard magical practices; some believe in the truth of the whole system, while others take the view that "whether the gods really exist is comparatively unimportant; the point is that the universe behaves as if they do". However the beliefs are held, the rituals of invocation call upon a 'god' to take possession of the devotee, so that he is completely identified with it; this is what a Christian would describe as demon possession. Having become unified with the 'god', the magician may then use its name to evoke a lesser spirit. The magical system envisages a hierarchy of spiritual beings, extending down from the Most High God to elemental spirits. Although God is addressed using the Biblical names of Jehovah, Adonai and Elohim, numerous other names are used, and God is not viewed as a person who wills good and abhors evil, but as a personification of Nature, 'beyond good and evil' and 'simply cosmic duality'. The power of the gods may be directed to good ('white') or evil ('black') purposes at the will of the magician.

The place of the will

In the magical system a central place is given to the power of the human will. Magical practitioners believe 'that human will power is a real force, capable of being trained and concentrated, and that the disciplined will is capable of changing its environment and producing supernatural effects'. They are prepared to go to quite extraordinary lengths to train the will, such as taking an oath to avoid using some common word, and self-inflicting a cut with a razor every time the oath is broken. The Scriptures reveal that such things were practised in the first century A.D., referring to "a show of wisdom in will-worship and humility, and severity to the body" (Colossians 2:23). Magicians hope that by so disciplining their will they will be able to direct elemental forces at their command.

The material world

Although there is no complete consistency, the magical system tends to see matter as evil, whereas the spiritual world is good. This idea is also shared by some pseudo-Christian cults, and is no new thing. The Gnostic heresy in the first century introduced it into Christian churches, and the apostle Paul wrote against it in the letter to the Colossians: "Take heed lest there shall be any one that maketh spoil of you through his philosophy and vain deceit, after the tradition of men, after the elements of the world, and not after Christ: for in Him dwelleth all the fulness of the Godhead bodily" (Colossians 2:8 RVM). This scripture emphasizes the bodily existence of Christ, and no Christian can accept the idea that matter is evil, since the Lord Himself is in bodily form. Modern magical writers point with approval to the Gnostic teachings as an example of the accommodation of a conventional religion to existing practices, but it is quite obvious that the apostles never tolerated this as legitimate. Timothy was urged to turn "away from the profane babblings and oppositions of the knowledge which is falsely so called", and it is apparent that pure Christian doctrine was threatened by the tendency of some to bring in heathen beliefs in the guise of spiritual knowledge.

In the Upper Room, the Lord Jesus instructed His disciples to take the bread and wine and give thanks for them, as He had done, as a remembrance of Himself. This simple act has been developed by some churches in Christendom into a ceremony in which it is taught that the bread and wine are transformed into the actual body and blood of the Lord, of which the worshippers then partake. Present-day writers on magic claim, possibly with some justification, that the idea of the mass is an adaptation to Christian beliefs of a much older ceremony in which "the magician invokes the god, thereby transmuting the material basis, then consumes the sacrament, and absorbs the energy and virtues of that god". Heathen rites of this sort have been revived, and 'witches sabbaths' are held today in which 'nature gods' are invoked. To make the participants feel at one with nature, rites may be carried out in which the participants are naked, and sometimes sexual unions between those taking part are involved.

Some heathen rites may resemble aspects of worship in Christendom, but they are not deliberate parodies of it. The rites of Satanism proper, on the other hand, are a deliberate attempt to parody the Mass. A writer on magic says "Satanists... are in reality as staunchly Christian as those who celebrate the real mass. Their rites, beliefs and practices are all modelled around the Christian religion ... So in a way one could say that Satanists, worshipping a Christian devil, are in fact as religious as the most orthodox Christian. What the Satanist is saying is that he feels betrayed by Christian churches ... he has seen no relief from his spiritual burdens". Satanists enact blasphemous sacrifices, say prayers backwards, and spit at the cross to show their hatred of Christ and God; yet they must believe that the God they reject is real, and deliberately take the side of Satan as His enemy. Undoubtedly, many relish the tang of evil, and gain a perverted pleasure from such defiance of God.

Frauds, fools or fiends?

It is obvious that all of the practices reviewed are opposed to Scriptural teaching, which condemns, in both Old and New Testaments, any attempt to communicate with spirits or Satan. It is difficult to determine the extent to which there is real communication with spirits by modern magicians. Practices of divination by various means may be mere devices to make money from the gullible, like fairground fortune-tellers and newspaper horoscopes. Their practitioners may deceive themselves as well as others, and honestly believe in the efficacy of what they do. It is tragic that the decline in soundly based Christian faith in Western countries has opened the door to superstition of all sorts. It is ironical that people who think that simple faith in Christ is childish, but who will not take the trouble to study Christian doctrine more deeply, will devour any half-baked ideas about the 'paranormal.'

There is some fraud, and more foolishness, in magical practices, but no Christian will deny that the "spiritual hosts of wickedness" (Ephesians 6:12) really do exist, and that they are capable of influencing, or even possessing, human beings. For this reason occult practices are not to be trifled with. Contempt for the mystic gibberish in which these things are enshrouded should not obscure the fact that a man who offers himself to a 'god' as a willing subject may find that the offer is taken up, with results that will be spiritually disastrous to him. The service of Satan or any of his inferiors will lead to the judgement designed for the master. Even in this life it may lead to an unsound mind and a depraved manner of life, as some of the sensational newspapers bear witness.

The antidote

The only effective antidote to the poison of Satan is Christ Himself. In reading occult literature, one is struck by the fact that although writers often refer to God and the gods, they have no place for Christ. All the elements of the gospel are needed to oppose occult teachings: the holiness of God, the fact of sin against Him, the need for a Redeemer, the deity and manhood of Christ, His atoning death, His bodily resurrection, and the need for faith in Him. The squalor and obscurity of the magical system are revealed in the light of the rational clarity of the revelation of God in Christ. Some men will deliberately choose the darkness, but it is the Christian's duty and privilege, by the help of the Holy Spirit, to bring to men who have been deceived by 'doctrines of demons' the light of the gospel of Christ.

9

THE MAN OF SIN (GEORGE PRASHER)

Dominant Personality of the End Time

The darkest era of human history has yet to be! Described by Daniel the prophet as "the appointed time of the end" (Daniel 8:19) it will occupy the seven years immediately before the coming to earth of the Lord Jesus as King of kings and Lord of lords (Revelation 19:11 - 16). That dark era will be dominated by "the man of sin", 'the son of perdition", "the lawless one" (2 Thessalonians 2:3, 8). Through him Satan will bring to fulfilment his age-long objective world acknowledgement of his supremacy in opposition to God and His Christ. Fittingly therefore the man of sin is also called the antichrist (1 John 2:1 8-22), for he will dispute the place given by the Father to our Lord Jesus, claiming for himself universal allegiance and worship.

Impressions of this outstanding person, the man of sin, the antichrist, are given in many prophetic scriptures dealing with the time of the end. The picture which emerges is sinister indeed! A contemptible person, he obtains power by flatteries (Daniel 11:21), speaks lies in political conference (v.27), perverts by flatteries (v.32). In Daniel 8 he is featured as a "king of fierce countenance, and understanding dark sentences" (v.23). Ruthlessly he treads other rulers underfoot to grasp power for himself (7: 19). Regardless of traditional religions or the desire of women, he magnifies himself above all (11:37). He does not scruple to slay millions who refuse to bow to his claims (Revelation 7:9-14).

The source of his authority and power

"His power shall be mighty, but not by his own power" is the brief but telling comment in Daniel 8:24. The apostle Paul amplifies this: "Then shall be revealed the lawless one... even he, whose coming is according to the working of Satan with all power and signs and lying wonders, and with all deceit of unrighteousness for them that are perishing" (2 Thessalonians 2:8-10).

World government under Satanic control is depicted in Revelation 12:3 by "a great red dragon, having seven heads and ten horns, and upon his head seven diadems". For Satan could validly say to the Lord Jesus, having shown Him all the kingdoms of the world in a moment of time, "To Thee will I give all this authority, and the glory of them: for it hath been delivered unto me: and to whomsoever I will I give it" (Luke 4:6). He is "the prince of this world" (John 12:31).

World government during the final phase of the man of sin's rule is depicted in Revelation 13:1,2 by a beast "having ten horns and seven heads, and on his horns ten diadems". The diadems formerly seen on the heads of the dragon are now seen on the horns of the beast. These horns represent ten kings who will receive authority with the beast, the man of sin (Revelation 17:12). Their adornment with the diadems illustrates the delegation of this immense authority and power by Satan: "The dragon gave him his power, and his throne, and great authority" (13:2).

The basis of his political power

The prophetic scriptures consistently identify the man of sin with a political power base in the area formerly controlled by the ancient Roman Empire. For example, the four beasts described in Daniel chapter 7 seem clearly to answer to the Babylonian, Medo-Persian, Grecian and Roman Empires, in that order. The fourth beast, representing the Roman power, had ten horns, among which arose another horn: the interpretation given in vv.24-28 shows that the dominant ruler so represented will encounter the Most High at the time when His everlasting kingdom will be ushered in. From which we understand that in the time of the end there will be a resurgence of a political power, answering to the former Roman Empire, and the man of sin will become its leading figure. Under his leadership the area will be controlled by ten kings, who receive authority with the man of sin: "these have one mind, and they give their power and authority unto the beast" (Revelation 17:12,13).

Again in Daniel 8 we see the Grecian Empire under Alexander the Great represented by the he-goat with a notable horn. After the he-goat overcame the ram with two horns (representing the

Medo-Persian Empire), the he-goat's great horn was broken. In its place Daniel saw four notable horns, representing, we understand, the four generals among whom Alexander's empire was divided. Then we are told that out of one of these four horns came forth a little horn which "waxed exceeding great" (v.9): in verses 23-25 the interpretation relates this "little horn" to the supreme end-time ruler, from which we learn that the man of sin will arise from one of the four areas into which Alexander the Great's empire was divided. Most of these were, of course, within the overall area later controlled by the Roman Empire.

Historical trends would not have encouraged the idea that the former area of the Roman Empire would again become the centre of gravity of world power. Were it not for divine revelation on the subject, other nations would have seemed to us more likely to achieve supremacy. Yet in quite recent times we have witnessed the growth of political consciousness towards European unity, based on the Treaty of Rome. Many students of Scripture regard this trend as an early phase of development towards the ten-kingdom confederacy in the ancient Roman Empire area, which Scripture predicts will be the basis of Antichrist's political and military power. From this power base he will dominate the world.

His blasphemous claims

Satan will incite the man of sin to oppose and exalt himself against all that is called God or that is worshipped, so that he will sit in the temple of God, setting himself forth as God (2 Thessalonians 2:4). These blasphemous claims reflect Satan's original folly, when as the anointed cherub on the holy mount of God he walked up and down in the midst of the stones of fire (Ezekiel 28:14); when he said in his heart, "I will ascend into heaven, I will exalt my throne above the stars of God… I will be like the Most High" (Isaiah 14:13, 14). In similar spirit, the man of sin, the lawless one, "speaking great things" (Daniel 7:8), will "speak words against the Most High" (7:25). He will "magnify himself in his heart" (8:25). He will "exalt himself and magnify himself above every god, and shall speak marvellous things against the God of gods" (11:36). There will be "given to him a mouth speaking great things and blasphemies"; and he will open his mouth "for blasphemies against God, to blaspheme His Name, and His tabernacle, even them that dwell in heaven" (Revelation 13:5,6).

His death-stroke healed

John's vision in Revelation 13:3 refers to the man of sin in terms of one of the heads of the beast seen coming up out of the sea: "I saw one of his heads as though it had been smitten unto death; and his death-stroke was healed: and the whole earth wondered after the beast; and they worshipped the dragon, because he gave his authority unto the beast; and they worshipped the beast, saying, Who is like unto the beast?" What is implied by this "death-stroke" may seem obscure, but both in Revelation 11:7 and 17:8 reference is made to the "beast that cometh up (or is about to come up) out of the abyss". Ezekiel also prophesied about the "deadly wounded wicked one… whose day is come, in the time of the iniquity of the end" (Ezekiel 21:25). It does therefore seem that Satan will have power to restore the man of sin from an apparently fatal wound, reinstating him in authority, and using the phenomenon to convince millions that they should worship both the man of sin and Satan himself Indeed it would seem that the whole episode will be a deliberate imitation of the death and resurrection of the Lord Jesus in order to establish Satanic claims to man's allegiance and worship.

His false prophet

A second beast is described in Revelation 13:11, having "two horns like unto a lamb, and he spake as a dragon". This we understand to represent the false prophet spoken of in Revelation 16:13 and 19:20, an evil genius devoted to the promotion of the worship of the first beast, whose death stroke was healed (13:12). The false prophet displays spectacular signs (v.13), deceiving them that dwell on the earth by reason of the signs which it was given him to do in the sight of the beast. He will be the ultimate fulfilment of the Lord's warning in Matthew 24:24: "False prophets ... shall show great signs and wonders; so as to lead astray, if possible, even the elect". He will command the making of an image to the man of sin who had the stroke of the sword and lived. He will even give breath to the image, causing it to speak. As many as will not worship the image will be killed. He will also order all to have a mark on their hand or forehead, the mark of the beast. Without it none will be allowed to buy or sell (Revelation 13:14-18).

His destruction of the "Great Harlot"

In Revelation 17 John vividly describes the Great Harlot, sitting on a scarlet coloured beast, full of names of blasphemy; having seven heads and ten horns. This would seem to depict the world religious system supported by the political system under man of sin's control. For it appears that he will patronise the apostate world religion during the first three and a half years of his power. Then he will "hate the harlot, and shall make her desolate and naked, and shall eat her flesh, and shall burn her utterly with fire" (17:16). This will be in harmony with his claim to worship from all mankind; no rival religious worship will be tolerated.

His attitude to Israel

As with the "harlot" of apostate world religion, so with the Israel nation, the man of sin will first conciliate and patronise. He will make a firm covenant for one week (seven years) with many, as we learn from Daniel 9:27. He will pervert many of Israel by flatteries (Daniel 11:32). So will the Lord's words be fulfilled: "I am come in My Father's name, and ye receive Me not; if another shall come in his own name, him ye will receive" (John 5:43). Then in the middle of the week (i.e. after 3 1/2 years) he will renounce the covenant. With dramatic sacrilege he will sit in the temple of God, setting himself forth as God. "For the half of the week he shall cause the sacrifice and the oblation to cease; and upon the wing of abominations shall come one that maketh desolate" (Daniel 9:27). About this the Lord Jesus gave clear warning to the God-fearing of Israel: "When therefore ye see the abomination of desolation, which was spoken of by Daniel the prophet, standing in the holy place ... let them that are in Judea flee unto the mountains... For then shall be great tribulation, such as hath not been from the beginning of the world until now, no, nor ever shall be" (Matthew 24:15-21).

Defiance of Almighty God

Satan, the man of sin and the false prophet have been well described as a "trinity of evil". In Revelation 16:13,14, we read that three unclean spirits were seen by John coming out of their mouths - spirits of demons working signs; which go forth unto the kings of the whole world, to gather them together unto the war of the great day of God, the Almighty. Through the man of sin, Satan will marshal the resources of his world-wide kingdom "against the LORD, and against His anointed, saying, Let us break their bands asunder, and cast away their cords from us ... He that sitteth in the heavens shall laugh: the Lord shall have them in derision" (Psalm 2:2-4). Coming forth as King of kings and Lord of lords, He will bring to nought the lawless one by the manifestation of His coming (2 Thessalonians 2:8). Both the beast and the false prophet will be cast alive into the lake of fire. "The Dragon, the old serpent, which is the Devil and Satan" will be bound and cast into the abyss for a thousand years (Revelation 19:19-20:3).

So the dazzling Satanic kingdom of the man of sin will be crushed by the Stone cut out of the mountain without hands (Daniel 2:45). In triumphant anticipation of this, let us delight in the Spirit's assurance: "The God of peace shall bruise Satan under your feet shortly" (Romans 16:20).

10

SATAN BRUISED UNDER OUR FEET (BRIAN FULLARTON)

In every sphere in heaven and on earth the Lord Jesus Christ will have supremacy. This has been the divine intention throughout the ages. In the present declining world situation the dream of universal turning to God as the result of faithful and sustained Christian preaching and testimony is not destined to realization. The totality of political chaos and religious apostasy in future times will only be removed by the intervention and judgement of Almighty God.

Satan is the worst rebel in the universe, prime instigator of all evil both in heavenly places and on earth. His insolent opposition has been tolerated in divine forbearance. But the end of that forbearance is in sight. The career of this exalted transgressor and great disturber of the nations is nearing its finale' as the first prophetic utterance given in Eden (Genesis 3:15) nears fulfilment. He who at one time was the chief executive and custodian of the rights of the throne of deity will have as his permanent dwelling the lake of fire. The principal offender of the created universe will be the greatest sufferer eternally. The contemplation of descent from his former residence in inconceivable majesty (Ezekiel 28 and Isaiah 14) to his final place in unimaginable degradation is fearful. Romans 16:20 assures us that "the God of peace shall bruise Satan under your feet shortly".

A Pre-millennium Judgement

The events of the opening verses in Revelation 20 are the natural and expected consequences of the momentous descent of the King of kings to earth, so graphically described in the previous chapter. The great political and religious leaders of Satan's doomed world empire, the Beast and the False Prophet, are smitten by one stroke and transported alive to their place of eternal punishment (Revelation 19:20). These two henchmen of Satan had wielded their power autocratically. Men and women in the world who had at first been grateful for their strong-handed dealings in government now prove by bitter experience that they committed themselves to a more galling tyranny than ever known before. The reign of terror of the Beast and the False Prophet will be abruptly terminated by the Lord's appearing from heaven.

Two Old Testament men, Elijah and Enoch were taken to heaven without dying, to share in eternal glory and joy. Here two men are summarily consigned to share torment forever without death or resurrection. The preparatory step to the establishing of Christ's millennial kingdom is the apprehending and committal of the Dragon - the evil genius and master criminal - to 'the abyss'. This period of imposed isolation will last for a thousand years. It is virtually impossible to visualize a world, exempt from Satan's policies and cruelties, enjoying the benign and righteous administration of God's Son. John the apostle states precisely his vision of the arch foe; 'laid hold on', 'bound', 'cast', "that he should deceive the nations no more, until the thousand years should be finished."

Three symbols of divine authority - a key, a chain and a seal - ensure that the devil will have no access or influence upon earth. His fiendish plans and diabolical deeds stain the annals of human history. The climax of his work was revealed in the murder of the Prince of Life. With the removal of the Church at Christ's coming, and consequently much of the Holy Spirit's activity, Satan will infiltrate every region of human society with great success. Now he is captive. 'The key' opens and closes the abyss; 'the chain' fetters Satan. No longer will his intelligence and malignity have free rein. 'The abyss' is a term used of a defined abode distinct from the 'lake of fire.' The word occurs nine times in the New Testament (Luke 8:31; Romans 10:7; Revelation 9:1,2&11; 11:7;17:8; 20:1&3). It is not figurative language. In most passages it signifies the place of captivity of demon spirits though in others it identifies the place of the departed.

The term 'dragon' depicts Satan controlling earth's political empires. He seduces men from God in his character as the 'old serpent'. He is also the devil, the father of lies, and as Satan he is the malignant and implacable adversary of God and man. World-wide peace will be the product of his imprisonment or 'binding' (Revelation 20:2). A binding of Satan took place at Golgotha. There is a clear reference to the triumphant victory of the cross in the words of Matthew 12:29. That binding was relative in the sense that Satan's house was spoiled, his power to hurt through the fear of death those who belong to Christ was dissipated and his fate was sealed. But he was not shut up from activity. While at present he cannot touch the eternal security of believers in the Lord Jesus he can wreck their spiritual lives. In the coming time he will be powerless to stupefy and afflict the nations. The strong angel, by divine command, shuts and seals the only entrance and exit of the abyss. He who once caused a seal to be placed upon the tomb of the Son of God has now a seal affixed upon his own domain.

The Millennium Period

No longer can Satan's evil deceptions drug the nations of earth. Whatever pockets of rebellion and outbreaks of immorality occur during the devil's incarceration will certainly not be directly attributable to him. Christ's reign with His own for a thousand years is a prelude to His everlasting kingdom (Revelation 22:5). The whole scene lies plainly across the page of Scripture of which Revelation 20:4-6 is a small part. This era of peace and prosperity was anticipated by Old Testament prophets and foreshadowed in the transfiguration of the Son of Man (Matthew 16:27, 28; 17:1-8).

The view that the Millennium will be a perfect state is based on supposition. Certainly rebellion will be dealt with summarily (Isaiah 65:20), but man on his final probation even under the most favourable conditions will demonstrate the irremediable corruption of the flesh. At the end of the thousand years Satan is released and stages a last but short-lived coup only to meet his final doom - the lake of fire - from which there is no reemergence. This will be the precursor of the time described in 1 Corinthians 15:24.

A Last-ditch Effort

During the final rebellion the mastermind of deceit will again manipulate those who flock to his standard. He will have world-wide support - "the four corners of the earth" (Revelation 20:8). The words 'God and Magog' represent the nations. They are not to be confused with references in Ezekiel 38 and 39 where events take place prior to the thousand-year reign in the invasion of Israel's territory by confederate powers. Satan's imprisonment had not made the slightest change in his implacable hatred of God.

This vast conspiracy gathers momentum. It is earth's final revolt against the Lord and His Christ. Gigantic effort it may be, against the "camp of the saints" (20:9) that is, the millennial saints, and "the beloved city" Jerusalem, but retribution is swift and decisive. Man's vaunted strength when directed against the Omnipotent is futile, even when planned by the skill and power-play of the devil. Animosity towards 'the land' has been consistent through the centuries. Pogrom-minded nations have been, are, and will be ignorant of God's purposes centred there.

The final means of judgement upon men who choose eternal death rather than life will be conflagration from heaven. "Fire from the Lord" consumed two companies of fifty men on a misguided mission, two hundred and fifty presumptuous rulers in Israel and two priests, the sons of Aaron. Those who have participated in the final affront to heaven after the millennium will be among the dead, the great and the small of Revelation 20:12 with the triumvirate of evil sharing the same end – the eternal fire spoken of by the Lord in Matthew 25:41.

The Abode of Eternal Suffering

The lake of fire is synonymous with Gehenna (Luke 12:5). It is the place of eternal suffering and endless remorse. Somewhere in God's universe a restricted area is prepared for sin's last judgement. No sin will take place in the lake of fire even though the hearts of the sufferers, having chosen their own destruction, remain sinful. Neither repentance nor new birth are possible there. Total subjection will be divinely enforced (1 Corinthians 15:25). Eternal punishment is solemnly mentioned by the Lord Jesus in Mark 9. Their worm does not die (the unceasing existence of the personality) and "fire is not quenched" (the unceasing inflicting of torture by fire as the instrument of judgement).

How different Satan's path has been from that of his Conqueror! The Self-Existent Son of God willingly took the lowest place and has been awarded the highest honour. Satan, the most wretched being of all God's creation, will suffer most in that place of absolute and eternal separation from the God of unchangeable holiness. He has successfully deceived the unbelieving into accepting the theory of non-eternal punishment and implanting doubts as to the eternal security of those who trust in the Christ. "Day and night" (Revelation 20:10) describes perennial perdition. There is no doctrine of annihilation in the Bible.

In view of these things how important it is to have a right understanding of Christ's eternal Sonship, His present Lordship and future Kingship. For the advent of Him "Who is the blessed and only Potentate, the King of kings and Lord of lords" we earnestly wait.

11

THE BELIEVER'S PRESENT STANDING (TOM HYLAND)

Throughout the centuries of man's history a mysterious evil power has wielded a profound influence in his affairs. Of this the evidence is irrefutable, and present world trends amply verify man's inability to free himself from it. This evil power is identified in Scripture as the awesome celestial being whose career and aspirations have been reviewed here in earlier chapters. Former contributors to this book have explored in some detail the biblical treatment of this momentous subject. Thoughtful readers, no doubt, have been impressed afresh with its gravity and its practical bearing on Christian life and service.

With this, as with all other facets of divine revelation, it is necessary to discipline our minds to accept with unquestioning faith what is written. And where Scripture is silent we must not resort to speculation. The careful expositor strives to hold the balance of revealed truth. Keeping this in mind it is apparent that any survey of the history of redemption which underrates or distorts Satan's crucial role in the great conflict of the ages will be found wanting.

The scope of Satanic aspirations

For the administration of His universe the Most High delegates certain powers to an order of celestial beings created for this purpose. They are named in Scripture "principalities and powers", their activities being controlled and harmonized according to the Creator's will. The Biblical record indicates that among these exalted beings a foremost place was assigned to Satan who was endowed with the highest intelligence and all the necessary powers befitting such high office.

In the counsels of Deity the Son of God is the appointed Heir of all things (Hebrews 1:2). As such He is the Head of all principality and power (Colossians 2:10). In Him the entire universe subsists. The ineffable glory of His Person and office was answered by the adoration of the entire heavenly host until an insidious rebellion inspired by Satan took shape. The scale and consequences of that rebellion were catastrophic. It led those who conceived it to cast off the restraints prescribed by the Creator and to aspire to forbidden heights. Satan's ultimate ambition is the dethronement of the Son of God so that he can capture for himself the allegiance and disposition of the entire creation. Such are the cosmic proportions of the conflict between God and His inveterate adversary. The issue can never be in doubt, but the course of the conflict is master-minded through its various stages by the triune God.

The Tragedy of Eden

Satan's traitorous ambitions brought swift and overwhelming judgement. The incarnate Christ portrayed that fateful event with one brief yet potent comment: "I beheld Satan fallen as lightning from heaven" (Luke 10:18). This did not imply that he was deprived of all his powers. Although expelled from high office among the heavenly hierarchy Satan and the vast host of spirits who joined in his rebellion were permitted to inhabit the earth and the air. From that vantage point he directs his kingdom of darkness in opposition to God's kingdom of light, still nursing the delusion that he can eventually outwit his Creator.

As we have already observed, the Satanic rebellion had cosmic consequences. But it transpired that the planet earth was to be the arena for the battle to be joined. The stage was set when the first man was installed as head of his earthly domain. Satan calculated that if he could capture Adam's allegiance and gain a foothold in his territory then mankind would fall under his sway. This daring and wicked enterprise was conceived and executed with characteristic cunning. The details of the Serpent's tactics in Eden need not detain us here. They have been carefully scrutinized in an earlier article in this series. Suffice it to say that what Satan imagined was his masterstroke proved to be his fatal blunder. There would be another Man another day. From the ruin of Eden God surveyed the centuries of human history and looked on to Bethlehem, to Gethsemane, to Gabbatha, to Golgotha, and to new heavens and a new earth purged from every trace of the Serpent's trail.

The guilty pair, crestfallen, were driven from the divine presence. But not without assurance of eventual deliverance; their adversary would one day meet his Conqueror:

> Soon as the reign of sin began
> The light of mercy dawned on man,
> When God announced the early news,
> "The woman's Seed thy head shall bruise."

It was as though the Son of God, the eternal Word and Heir of all things, with compassionate love said, I will go after them and provide the way by which the banished ones may be brought back to My Father.

The Triumph of Golgotha

One glorious day it happened! Rising from His throne in unapproachable light, the Son of God laid aside the garments of imperial majesty and, by birth from a human mother, entered His own world. This was the Event of the ages. Creation waited for it, wise men and prophets longed to see it, angels desired to look into it. At the time, in the place, and in the manner prescribed in the prophetic word the Redeemer had come "that He might destroy the works of the devil" (1 John 3:8). Every step of His pathway was dogged by the evil one. But the tempter could gain no advantage over the second Man. As Satan deployed all his forces, spiritual and human, for the decisive battle, the sinless undefiled Son of Man announced to His apostles, "The prince of the world cometh: and he hath nothing in Me" (John 14:30).

Satan's victory over the first man exposed all mankind to the Creator's righteous wrath. There was, however, a means by which that wrath could be averted - by the sacrifice of a sinless victim who could "bear the wrath to sinners due". Thus only could God's claims be vindicated and man retrieved from the bondage of sin and Satan. This was the crux of the Redeemer's mission, and Satan's strategy was to divert Him from it at that critical late hour. At Golgotha the battle-lines were drawn. On the one side stood Satan, the author of evil; on the other, the Lord's Anointed, the Heir of all things:

> "Earth trembles in the scale,
> Yet knows not of the fight,
> And if her fearful foe prevail,
> It will be always night."

Glorious victory! Battle-scarred, yet completely in command, the lonely Sufferer vanquished His adversary and paid the ransom price. All Satan's ambitions received their death blow. "When the Man on the centre cross suddenly raised His resolute eyes to the sky, and cried, 'It is finished' the whole kingdom of darkness must have trembled to its foundations."

Although Satan's defeat took place on Golgotha's hill the Saviour's cry of victory resounded in the far distances of the universe. The apostle Paul described the extent of the finished work of Christ with the words, "having made peace through the blood of His cross" (Colossians 1:20). The context of that phrase indicates that through the Saviour's sacrificial death harmony will be restored to the entire creation. Every discordant note introduced by Satan will be eliminated forever and the old serpent banished to the lake of fire. Such will be the far-reaching consequences of the Redeemer's reconciling work. It is the divine purpose "to sum up all things in Christ" (Ephesians 1:10). Then at long last, and for eternity, God will "be all in all" (1 Corinthians 15:28).

"In Christ" - A new Creation

From New Testament revelation we learn that the Redeemer's victory had retrospective consequences for mankind of former ages (see e.g. Romans 3:25; Hebrews 2:14,15). And the future of the nation of Israel, as well as much else arising from God's dealings with mankind in past ages, comes within the framework of the total triumph at Golgotha. In studying Scripture treatment of our subject this telescopic view should always be given its place. But in closing this article we look specifically at the bearing of the Second Man's victory in terms of divine-human relationships in the present age.

Adam's fall into sin was not something affecting him alone. He was federal head of the human race from whom we all inherit a sinful status. The sins we commit as individuals arise from, and are proof of our state of alienation from God transmitted to us from Adam. This solidarity of mankind with its federal head lies at the base of the apostle Paul's reasoning in Romans 5:12-21. There he compares man's standing in Adam with the believer's standing in Christ. Adam was a figure (type) of Him that was to come. Both Adam and Christ transmitted to their posterity the consequences of a single decisive act. Adam's one trespass brought all his offspring under the dominion of sin and death. The Second Man by one act of obedience transmits His perfect righteousness' to all united to Him as their federal Head. When a child of Adam comes to Christ in repentance and faith he is delivered out of the power of darkness, and translated into the kingdom of the Son of God's love (Colossians 1:13).

This glorious concept captivated the mind and heart of Paul during his first Roman imprisonment. To summarize all that has been secured for the believer through his identification with his Saviour the apostle brings into service the term "in Christ". In the opening verses of Ephesians I the stream of divine grace is traced back to its source: we were chosen "in Christ" before the foundation of the world. Then the apostle follows the revitalizing stream as it flows down to Adam's sinful posterity through the triumph of Golgotha: "we have our redemption through His blood, the forgiveness of our trespasses, according to the riches of His grace". Finally, he identifies the moment when the virtue of the covenant Sacrifice is credited to each believer: "in whom (Christ) ... having heard the word of the truth, the gospel of your salvation, - in whom, having also believed, ye were sealed with the Holy Spirit of promise, which is an earnest of our inheritance."

Satan is powerless to touch our new standing "in Christ": "your life is hid with Christ in God", wrote Paul to the Colossians (3:3). "In Christ" the believer is endowed with a new quality of manhood which will be fully manifested in due course: "we shall be like Him; for we shall see Him even as He is" (1 John 3:2):

> "Like Him in all those lovely traits,
> Which in His lowly, earthly days

So beautiful we see."

This moral transformation will coincide with the bodily change which is the crown of our new standing "in Christ": "we wait for a Saviour... who shall fashion anew the body of our humiliation, that it may be conformed to the body of His glory" (Philippians 3:20,21).

"What then shall we say to these things?"

At the conclusion of this brief study of a captivating theme, Paul's challenge has a particular relevance. The dimension of the Redeemer's victory over our infamous foe, in its conception and execution, brings us face to face with the nobility of our calling. We belong to a new age which the world takes no account of. Yet we are required in our present lives to transmit the characteristics of our new status "in Christ" in terms of human conduct. "I therefore ... beseech you" pleaded Paul, "to walk worthily of the calling wherewith ye were called, with all lowliness and meekness" (Ephesians 4:1,2). The exhortation touches us all. Laxity in Christian conduct is all too obvious in this superficial age. The corrective is assimilation, by faith and holy contemplation, of the true nature of our calling. As the Spirit of God enlightens and animates our minds there will be a shining through in our manner of life: "Every one that hath this hope set on Him purifieth himself, even as He is pure" (1 John 3:3).

12

THE BELIEVER'S PRESENT RESOURCES (HENDY TAYLOR)

"What then shall we say to these things? If God is for us, who is against us? He that spared not His own Son, but delivered Him up for us all, how shall He not also with Him freely give us all things?" (Romans 8:31-32).

From the study of this subject over the course of this book, three important conclusions have emerged. Firstly, that the forces of evil led by the malignant genius of Satan should not be under-estimated, they must be faced and never ignored. Secondly, that God is stronger than His foes; the work of Christ at Calvary has overcome him who had the power of death, that is the Devil (Hebrews 2:14). Thirdly, that God in His grace and wisdom has, through the power of the Holy Spirit, provided us with the resources and the means to withstand the forces of evil in our spiritual lives. It is to the last of these assertions that this concluding chapter of the series is addressed.

The imprisoned apostle was moved by the Holy Spirit to describe these resources as the whole armour of God (Ephesians 6:11-18). Perhaps as he gazed upon the Praetorian guard who kept watch over him, the integral parts of his armour developed in his mind a deep spiritual significance:

(a) Loins girded with truth implies bracing oneself in readiness for active service for the Lord to maintain sincerity and reality by truthfulness, in contrast to hypocrisy and falsehood.

(b) The breastplate of righteousness refers to doing what is right. This is not imputed righteousness but as John says "He that doeth righteousness is righteous, even as He is righteous" (1 John 3:7). Doing wrong may appear at first to be successful but, as the Psalmist discovered, it has a sad conclusion (see Psalm 73:17-19).

(c) Feet shod with the preparation of the gospel of peace - the believer must be ready and prepared to spread the gospel of peace, his walk must be worthy of it and a testimony to those who receive the message.

(d) The shield of faith - the Roman shield was large and oblong and protected every part of the soldier. Faith can protect the whole of the Christian's activities and make him impervious to all the fiery darts of the Devil.

(e) The helmet of salvation - this speaks of divine deliverance. In every conflict salvation can be the present experience of believers.

(f) The sword of the Spirit the Word of God is a weapon which is both defensive and offensive. The Lord Jesus himself had recourse to the Word when opposed by the Adversary in the desert. The writer to the Hebrews tells us that the Word of God is "living, and active, and sharper than any two-edged sword, and piercing even to the dividing of soul and spirit, of both joints and marrow, and quick to discern the thoughts and intents of the heart" (Hebrews 4:12).

The effectiveness of these resources is totally dependent upon perseverance in prayer, not spasmodic or self-centred, but all prayer at all seasons for all saints. Truth, righteousness, peace, faith, salvation, the Word of God and prayer are seven vital features of the Christian's resource. To dispense with any of these is to invite defeat in the spiritual battle, for we must put on the whole armour.

If a believer is to be a good soldier of Christ Jesus, he must first learn that there is One to whose supreme authority he must bow. It is our responsibility to obey and also to exercise the authority delegated to us. We can nullify the cowardly activities of the Adversary. "Resist the Devil, and he will flee from you" (James 4:7). Spiritual 'warfare is not only defensive; there are occasions when the battle must be taken into the enemy's camp. This will be achieved, not by physical or political means, but by the preaching to the sinner of the gospel of the grace of God and to believers the message of the Kingdom of God.

When Jude wrote of contending earnestly for the Faith which was once for all delivered unto the saints (Jude 3), he envisaged that struggle and conflict would be an intrinsic part of Christian testimony during the present age. What is the Faith? It is the revealed will of God for His people expressed in a body of doctrine received and carried out by those who hold it. It is a deposit handed over to the saints to be stoutly defended.

The challenge can come not only from without but also from enemies within the churches. Jude speaks of ungodly men who have crept in secretly "turning the grace of our God into lasciviousness, and denying our only Master and Lord, Jesus Christ" (Jude 4). Paul gives a similar warning to the Ephesian elders at Miletus. "I know that after my departing grievous wolves shall enter in among you, not sparing the flock; and from among your own selves shall men arise, speaking perverse things, to draw away the disciples after them" (Acts 20:29-30). The infiltration of evil men and the destructive heresy of those false teachers undermined the testimony from within. Let us be warned.

The doctrines of the Faith have been under constant attack down through the centuries since the days of the apostles. The authority of Scripture and the vital doctrine of inspiration have been the subject of continuing controversy. The denial of the Deity and eternal Sonship of Christ represent major attacks upon Christian testimony. Other modern trends such as the feminist movement also play a part. What is our resource? None other than the Word of God, for the Faith is written. It must not be tampered with but practised, defended and passed on without modification - the whole counsel of God. The warrior for the Lord Christ may sometimes be called upon to stand alone but final victory is never in doubt.

The world today presents a picture which is depressing, disturbing and ugly. The violence and crime, especially of very young people, is a living proof of the doctrine of original sin and clear evidence that "the whole world lieth in the evil one" (1 John 5:19). The believer, however with the privilege of the divine perspective and possessing the resources that God has bountifully bestowed upon him can rejoice with Peter "that the proof of your faith, being more precious than gold that perisheth though it is proved by fire, might be found unto praise and glory and honour at the revelation of Jesus Christ: whom not having seen ye love; on whom, though now ye see Him not, yet believing, ye rejoice greatly with joy unspeakable and full of glory; receiving the end of your faith, even the salvation of your souls" (1 Peter 1:7-9).

When Israel, by divine command,
The pathless desert trod,
They found through all that barren land
A sure resource in God.
Like them we have a rest in view
Secure from adverse powers;
Like them we pass a desert too,
But Israel's God is ours.

ABOUT THE PUBLISHER

Hayes Press (www.hayespress.org) is a registered charity in the United Kingdom, whose primary mission is to disseminate the Word of God, mainly through literature. It is one of the largest distributors of gospel tracts and leaflets in the United Kingdom, with over 100 titles and many thousands dispatched annually. In addition to paperbacks and eBooks, Hayes Press also publishes Plus Eagles' Wings, a fun and educational Bible magazine for children, and Golden Bells, a popular daily Bible reading calendar in wall or desk formats.

If you would like to contact Hayes Press, there are a number of ways you can do so:

By mail: c/o The Barn, Flaxlands, Royal Wootton Bassett, Wiltshire, UK SN4 8DY

By phone: 01793 850598

By eMail: info@hayespress.org

via Facebook: www.facebook.com/hayespress.org

www.ingramcontent.com/pod-product-compliance
Lightning Source LLC
Chambersburg PA
CBHW071359130726
47996CB00002B/989